Published by: Ingrid Wilson (Experiments in Fiction)
Text Design by: Experiments in Fiction
Cover Art by: Kerfe Roig
Cover Design by: Experiments in Fiction
Illustrations by: Valdis Stakle
ISBN: 9798531987747

Ingrid Wilson (editor)
THE ANTHROPOCENE HYMNAL
an
Experiments in Fiction
Publication

For my children,
and all the children of the earth.

- I.W.

THE

ANTHROPOCENE HYMNAL

Ingrid Wilson (editor)

Contents

Why 'The Anthropocene Hymnal?'

The term 'Anthropocene' was coined by scientists in the Soviet Union as early as the 1960s, and then popularised by ecologist Eugene F. Stoermerin in the 1980s. In the year 2000 the term was used by atmospheric chemist Paul J. Crutzen to denote a new era: one in which man-made changes to the earth's atmosphere and ecosystems would show up in the fossil record. Over the last 80 years, scientists have come to realise that man-made technologies, agriculture and industry are having a detrimental effect upon the natural environment.

When I was growing up, in the 1980s and early 90s, we called it 'Global Warming.' This has since become 'Climate Change,' partially because warming is not the only effect we see from exponentially rising greenhouse gas emissions, but also, I suspect, because it sounds less ominous. 'Climate Change' is not necessarily man-made, and can therefore be conveniently ignored, or even denied, by political lobbyists from the many modern industries which devastate the natural environment. The PR machine stretches its tentacles throughout the whole earth, lulling us into a false sense of security before finally strangling us off the planet.

It has come to light recently that oil companies including Shell (oh, the irony of a name!) and Exxon predicted the effects of unchecked fossil-fuel consumption back in the 1980s, and since then did everything they could to cover up their own predictions. Now, in the early 2020s, the worst of these predictions are coming true: from vast wildfires to catastrophic floods, from decimation of insect life to global pandemic. There can be little doubt that we have now entered a self-defining era, the Anthropocene. We can only hope that we have not also initiated the sixth mass extinction of life on this planet.

Back in October of 2020, I started writing for a poetry forum called earthweal, the brainchild of David Cohea (writing under the pseudonym Brendan). I was moved by his weekly prompts and the variety of heartfelt responses to them, which consistently reminded me of the mess we are in, and also of the perils of giving in to apathy, or losing hope. To me, these poems are earth-songs and heart-songs. The 'poetry of a changing earth' (to use earthweal's tagline) is a unique response to an unprecedented crisis. I began to think that such songs might grow in strength should they be joined together in chorus. Out of this idea, 'The Anthropocene Hymnal' was born.

In my call for submissions, I asked for poetry responding to the twin crises of climate change and biodiversity loss. I was overwhelmed by the response, and the strength of feeling behind the poetry submitted. I also mined the earthweal archives and asked for permission from collaborators to feature their poetry in this book. My thanks to both David Cohea and Sherry Marr for the inspiration, and to all who submitted to this anthology or earthweal, joining their voices in song to make this collection possible. Special thanks are also due to Kerfe Roig, who provided the cover art, and Valdis Stakle, who provided the internal illustrations.

I have subtitled this collection 'songs of a self-defining era,' because to me, poetry is song without the need for any separate melody. When we read these poems, we hear their song within our hearts. And this is a self-defining era, because I believe that our actions at this crucial time will come to define us as a species, for better or worse. The collection reads as a hymnal, from the desperate cries with which the book begins, to the prayers and invocations of hope which form its conclusion.

Putting this collection together has been a true labour of love for me, and I hope you are as moved by the end result as I am. If these songs resonate with you, and you are moved by their message, please share this message with others.

- Ingrid Wilson (editor), June 2021

PART I

From Despair...

INGRID WILSON (ED.)

Slow Sleepwalk into Armageddon
by Ingrid Wilson

It was a sweet walk, where we once held hands
and danced;
a waltz around the wilting wheatfields
imagining that we still had a chance:
slow sleepwalk into Armageddon
like dying flames of a once-wild romance.

Slow sleepwalk into Armageddon like
a fevered dream
delirious and staggering
and tossed like whirling twigs within a stream
of consciousness,
unconscious of the brink to which we'd come

till we went over. Down and down we fell!
Some had the nerve to cry 'What have we done
to deserve this?'
While others knew the answer all too well:
Slowly, we'd sleepwalked into Armageddon,
transforming all the bounty of the Earth
into a living Hell.

Let's imagine we still have a chance:
Waltz with me...

When I come back, I will be grief
by Sherry Marr

We start out whole,
losing pieces of ourselves
along the way,
and then reclaiming them.
That is the journey.
I am collecting the last few bits,
before I fly into the light.
I pick them up:
- ah, there you are! -
and add them to my pack.

When I return,
I will change my shape.
I will be cattails,
standing dry, bent and broken
at the edge of the dried-up pond.
I will be wolf-pup,
peering fearfully from my den,
knowing, to survive,
I must elude Earth's biggest enemy:
the predatory Two-Leggeds,
and they are
everywhere.

I fear
I will find a planet burning,
humans and animals
on the run.
I will be Tree,
gasping for air,
a sudden irradiation
as the orange tongues
lick greedily at my corpse.
I will be lizard,
parching on the earth's
baked crust.

I will be deer,
fleeing the flaming forests.
I will be mother orca, holding
my dead newborn calf
above the water
for seventeen days, grieving,
unable to let her go,
saying to the humans:
See! See what you have done!

I will be grief itself,
watching the planet
that I love
burning itself up.
As I am now.
As I am now.

Destiny of this earth
by Gabriela Marie Milton

destiny of this earth
you are my destiny too
I burn in wildfires and spin in the eyewalls of hurricanes
that should never be
I sit at the intersection of two bridges that lead nowhere
wonder how many days this earth and I have left
there is no more laughter in the eyes of the stars
there are no more shells on the shore
the waves leave behind the deformed plastic of heated
summers
echoes of drunken voices
I vacillate between the poetry of broken glass and the
memory of winters
that do not exist anymore
metallic noises breathe the air
and eat from the shoulder of the mountain
a curse floats in the horizon

you
my earth
in autumn when I used to break the fruit of the vines
under my feet
you nursed me under your shades of green
dressed me in small shy roses
covered my face in the first dew of your mornings
now tell me

how to heal the wounds of your forests
placate the jaws of your non-ending storms
erase the negative of love from the face of your cries

destiny of this earth
you are my destiny too
teach me what saviors do

Blood-drop in Israel
by Ellie Onka

The birth of tragedy
like a maniac trembling
and she's a poet through withdrawals;

Leaving all behind,
the moon only knows death
under its eyes; was it his fault
or mine? Wastrels in the gardens grow
while we lay the feet of bone-frail
flowers
to the springsummer.

Like a paper on my skin
I swallow the air—the bed of gardens
whore themselves to death
in her womb; I walk away
I am the blood of his children
a sweat drop in Israel, and mother
is tarnished by ourselves; Neptune eyes
exalt
there is vanishing in the dénouement
and we'll lose by win of pseudopsychosis
elements of air and tragedy
her prime taunt
among death's leavetaking
floating through faces of the moon
inhaling mercury in its veins.

Save Your Tears for Another Day
by Jaya Avendel

The horizon blisters
the moon melts in the icicles
only the sun unwraps her cotton robe and
bathes in a copper basin filled with
diluted sweat. Today she
calls it seawater.

The darkness of the night is
crushing. Each star is a voice in
protest of a cruel dawn.

A cup of tea over brews
stains the china permanently with a milky glaze
a windowpane shatters because a
rock exploded and pattered its heart
In the wrong solar system.

The ocean dries down to the sand
an expanse of water stolen in the night
by a thirsty goddess
who cried.

Tea Time
by Tricia Sankey

the ocean-

a sinless mirror
peers up with
bleary eyes
see how she writhes
as you dip your feet -
carbon footprints
take
  a
   dive

stuck to the floor
you hear a
song -
there's nothing
wrong

the siren
sings -
she offers
you
  hot
   tea

Invocations
by Jane Dougherty

Night night go away
leave bristle bushes behind
to spike sow-thistled
drying brown stalks in withering sun

groundwater glares with Glaucus eyes
no saving us from drowning
we bend beneath the weight of the storm
ocean-pelted
reeds
will we rise again?

Running running away
filling earth's pockets with dull change
chinking over stream debris.

What magic will work
without sun to turn pewter to silver
pay our thirty pieces
open the valves and bivalves
drink up Thor's horn and make way below
for these cloud-fallen waters?

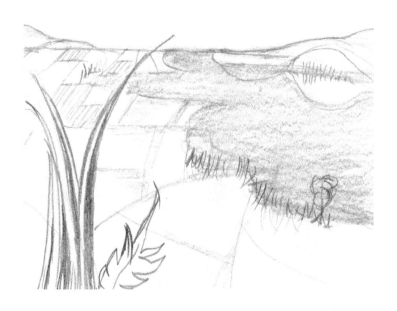

Whale Petroglyph
by David Cohea

Whales are gone from Sydney Harbour
but their ghosts sing to each other
in the petroglyphs widely scattered
around the water's rim. The etchers
are gone too but their music remains,
a pod of vowels chinked in long stone.

We had barely begun grieving whales
when the petroglyphs were connected
revealing the wild knowledge once here,
a cultural sooth of the mind's deep water,
spouts and flukes and crashings down
long cries in water and rebirthing song.

Hardly much recompense in a stone scratch
but ghosts throng wilder where a wild's
most extinct: Praise then to vast waters
empty now but for the dead mouth of reefs
too wide for oil spills and raining plastics.
Nights of such silence throng with ghost whales,
smashing and loving and feeding on grief.

Such breadth we'll never ken from shores
dynamited for bridges & dredged for docks
derricked with cruise ships and tankers,
tall condos fanning an opera house's shells.
But in the petroglyphs whales still run wild,
lost forever in glorious unglossed style.
Especially the carvings built over or drowned.

Mating and birthing pods of dark tongue
diving through dead nights in heavenly throng
feeding on an abundance equally inert.
Absence is loudest in grief's listening heart
kenning such faint bells in ancient rock art.
How profound the echoing distance of song
hallowed and deepened by knowing it's gone.

Waving Goodbye
by Kim Whysall-Hammond

Waves out to the immense horizon
roll rise fall
ancient beginnings echo
ocean, primal home
where life thrives
in hot plumes

Waves hide her dark deeps
where strange creatures lurk
living tubes metres long
angler fish
blind scrabbling crabs

Waves throw up on the shore
remnants of ocean lives
tangles of plastic
debris from both sides
of a blurring boundary
revealing hints of the diversity underneath
and of the death we impose

Waves swishing over
the black volcanic beach
erasing my footprints
we are all ghosts now

Amaryllis Interrupted

by Amber Fields

White these waves no longer crash upon the shore,
perhaps they don't deem themselves worthy—
the past between my teeth,
the future grim nowhere to be seen,
only, a handful of amaryllis bulbs remain, interrupted.
I think on some level we already knew,
as caskets of dormancy announce their arrival,
oh how these lips instigate the once green fields to ma-
terialize,
a savoring for days gone by— wispy clouds had fore-
warned,
tell me, did it stay unblemished for you?
The flame of my pen trembles at mere thought of the
world
reverting to ashes, of reverting
to ashes,
to ashes, to ashes,
to ashes alone we shall return.

Dirt Sky
by Diana Tenes

Earth crumbled rich dark, encrusted hands dig flicking
specks, chunks, earthworm parts, pincher
bugs,
life death darkness green, peeking out torn leaves, roots
filament
deciduous, cadaverous, cavernous
sun crackling leaves dried burnt burial lives lost
ancestors call drumming hills
hurt my ears
voices echo generations past
galaxies of stars, sprinkles planets shoot forth
loins ache hearts beat blood spurts drenches constella-
tions
I yearn to go back to where I was born from
where the past present future tumble to one place one
hole
that I found playing in the backyard as a child
that the dog peed in

Grounded

by Veronica Cassone McGowan

Branches hang heavy (like me)
drought, ice, snow, rain, wind
when will it stop?
Constant change
blowing from north then south
dizzying
sometimes crushing
it's getting hotter
unbearable
I know my time is coming
roots keep me grounded
I want to run

[don't tell me you're only visiting]
by Tan Ruey Fern

temporal fiction of a cherry blossom spring,

spliced with broken peals   of this sports car reckon-
ing

wreckage cries the wind no longer sing

of camera-action   on a sapling half-planted

the whims of wailing crowds like lightning

right or wrong? loved or   it doesn't matter

the banyans cannot balance on the violent swing

green to concrete grey   and leaves to
ashes

eternal fiction of a cherry blossom spring

curling red like a serpent   or a lie

so trace the mangrove root the body brings

the rhythm of the earth   is not a play

no monomythic stories these dream-rose things

i say we should dance of worms instead

of fruit bats of red soil of lifeblood instead.

The Wheatsheaf
by Ingrid Wilson

A whisper shakes the wheatfield
soft and sibilant;
someone's walked over my grave
this afternoon:
a whisper, a shiver
then silence echoes in my ear;
I feel that we've been here before.

For centuries we've sowed the fields
and ploughed the fields
and harvested the wheat:
The Wheatsheaf – quaint name
of a village pub.
I've never seen a Wheatsheaf
in real life; only the finished loaf.

Food comes to us
processed, packaged, and sanitised, though
our ancestors knew
bad harvest meant starvation
bad harvest was a thing to dread:
'Bring out number weight & measure in a year of
dearth'
the prophet said.

For years and years there were no years of dearth
but only plenty
over the whole earth
or at least
the part of it in which we lived
which meant the whole wide world, for all we cared:

children starved in Africa while
we sent money guiltily
and told our kids to eat their dinner
thinking 'this could never happen here;'
sure, as long as all the superstores stayed open
it could never happen here
but now

our house is on fire,
the flames are licking our back door;
bees are dying
crops are failing
disease and fear enough to empty shelves.
We talk about it down *The Wheatsheaf*
2 metres apart: 'but did you see the empty shelves?'

The fields, empty of wheatsheaves
ultimately lead to empty shelves:
our new-learned ignorance
means we have lost the instinct to survive.
Survival's not a game for politicians;
it's when you have to fill your empty stomach
for yourself.

A whisper shakes the wheatfield
soft and sibilant;
someone's walked over a mass grave
this afternoon:
a whisper, a shiver
then silence in echoes in the air:
it sighs and moans, with no-one left to hear.

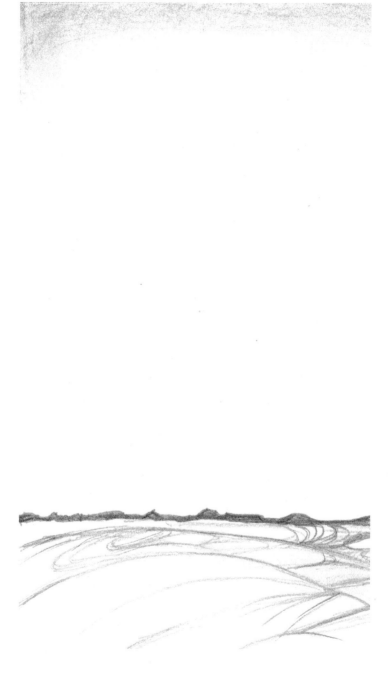

No Voice Speaks
by Merril D. Smith

When the ancient bough breaks and falls
in the forest of nevermore, lost
as wanderers once were
among the aged hardwood giants

the sea has swallowed
the coasts, and tongue-tied the towns, silencing them
forever--

while the trees further inland sway in swift-tailed winds,
singing and strumming the branches like guitar strings.
But strings break, and the wind changes key,
a new melody drifts
over the melted, bear-less arctic to vine-creeped cities

where cockroaches dance, and rats skitter-scratch
under the moon's silver-toned stream--
though no one is left to admire her argent beauty.

Dark in the Woods
by Peter Hague

It will be dark in the woods
when we re-enter its living space
after millenniums of streets
have fallen and failed.
When all we have left
is our lanterns and memories –
and the courage to listen
ourselves to sleep.

When we live amongst trees
we will grow the next stem,
we will unfold a new leaf
to replace our past.
We will learn to share
the simple devices
of art and philosophy,
where the darkness is healed.

There is a Lord of Souls
in the comforting woods
and we will come to know
the benefits of autumn –
when our souls have ceased
their civil reliance –
when all we have left
are lanterns and darkness.

Chirp
by Diana Tenes

Our expansive backyard contains nurturing trees
a statuesque Oak, a Palm with giant fronds, an Almond
swaying reaching delicate branches
a small slightly askew water fountain
an oval pond surrounded by sturdy rocks with concrete
merboy contemplating
a wood swing hanging from a branch like a giant strong
man's arm
an open wrought iron gazebo with flowering plants,
crawling beans and potted plant soldiers

Airborne visitors fly in, land in their places
bluejay, robin, woodpecker, sparrow, mockingbird,
finches, doves, hummingbirds
seagulls, ducks fly overhead, chickens live next door
butterflies do their windy dance
I am blessed to shelter this magical paradise

My bedroom window catches light, lies in wait
I strain to hear the sound of chirping in the morning
breath
it's time to wake when a bird echoes my ear, I long to
hear
sometimes there is a tiny chorus
sometimes it's one bird

I prepare the day I know I'll cry,
sob wretched
I expect
chirps
might
not
be

When we fall
by Jane Dougherty

The point turns when there is no reason.
The tipped balance will not be measured
in degrees numbers floods or fires.

The point is turned
darkness laps feet on the brink
when there is no more reason to long for spring
to look for nesting birds
listen for the thrush's song
no reason to watch the meadow
for the first hare.

The balance will tip in the silence
of absence of thrush and hare
when no fox trots the night sniffing the stars
when the last blackbird has sung his song
and slipped into memory.

When they have gone so has reason.

Where have all the Bees Gone?
by Liyona

Where have all the bees gone?
Singing lullabies to the
ancient trees as they shade the meadows
I hear the sweet soft
rumble of the honey fairies as they
pass me in the open
morning air.
Where have all the bees gone?
Flowers swaying in the meadows
full of life and color
have faded to pale and yellowed
hues
even the robin wonders about
his friendly neighbors.
Where have all the bees gone?
Circling and buzzing
breathing and feeding
but always giving
bringing a peace and rhythm to the world
hidden but
essential.
Where have all the bees gone?
I tell my child about
the stings and pricks
and how these
mighty kings
carried the memories

of mother earth on their
wings
how we miss them
for we are lost
will we find
our way back to
the rich and blossoming earth
when our guides have left?

The Bee-yond-Human Realm

by Sherry Marr

Small bee,
I hear you singing
your busy-nature song.
I wonder what the words are,
as you work the whole day long.
Do you sing praises to your queen,
or memories of the flower,
whose nectar so delighted you
in the early morning hours?
They say when your beekeeper dies,
someone tells you,
and you grieve.
"He is gone", they say,
and shroud your hive
in black, till you believe.
Such a small, diligent worker
on whose slight wings our future rests.
Seven billion souls you feed;
may your flight path
be blessed.

Silent Sky

by Ivor Steven

My morning sky is silent
an empty clear blue vent
a vast quietness
cloudless and soundless
the world has turned mute
we cannot hear
the whales crying
we no longer see
the birds flying
we now refuse to speak
words of peace, "Are they slowly dying?"
My morning sky has no sun
spent gold, overused, and undone
a grey dullness
viewless, a hollow darkness
the world has lost sight
we no longer see
industrious bees
we cannot hear
the animals fear
we now deny the people's voice
words of peace, our children's choice!

Scents of Eucalyptus
by Jude Itakali

"Here Lies Old Kaka!"
Pinned upon these walls,
of they who wrought her demise.

In years gone by
the scents of Eucalyptus would summon me
how tall Old Kaka was,
how vast her family.
In this valley,
an alcove of nature bloomed
beautiful and unclaimed
for Each, and for All
but now, no more.

Beneath Kaka's shade
amidst the hanging flora
Pike Pond resided
oh, the laughter by its banks!
And that moonlit orchid dance

a memory now lamented.

Critters in the grass
hoppers and crawlers alike
a lone child in awe
of the twilit firefly glee
and Jane, the ladybug queen

beauty and life our children will never see.

Oh, breath of nature
the scents of eucalyptus
fragrances unknown
this barren breeze reminds me
of a life that used to be

nature destroyed, with no one to atone.

To the greedy who destroy
I have much to say
but for us to find a way,
I will share my dismay:

Here lies Old Kaka
Here lies Pike Pond
Here, the ladybug died
Here, the fireflies fled
Here, the laughter is no more!

Dunston Checks Out

by Constance Bourg

Occupying the penthouse of the canopy, the King
of Ginger Swingers, Man of the Forest,
lived large. A two hundred pound bird
singing. Amusing with a thrust of his jaw
his jungle audience. And later on
the final place where you could see
his body lumbering, infecting with his yawn
a ragtag bunch of ennui brothers,

was in a glass box. And then there was one.
Studied, poked, prodded by mankind,
who pushed the final button and declared
this Titan of Apes to be blind, and while
the elevator sinks towards marble transience
we hold yet another impotent conference.

Turning Point
by Jim Feeney

If you listen carefully, sometimes,
you can hear paradigms shift.

In forests, plants share nutrients
through fungal networks.

Can a poem be a series
of seemingly unconnected sentences?

Dragging fishing nets across the ocean floor
releases large amounts of carbon dioxide
and acidifies the ocean;

carbonic acid, the most musical of all the acids.

A financial analyst writes an article
stating that the climate crisis
can only be solved by government regulation,
capitalism is not fit for the purpose.

We must put our foot down
to change our footprint.

Is that the sound of a paradigm shifting
a chair scraping back from the table

furniture moving in the room above.

When?

by Paul Vincent Cannon

When the last feather falls
we will bequeath our perfectly
designed lifestyles to microbes
as yet to evolve in the wastelands
of our creative imaginings, while
our self-congratulations will resound
at every vacant podium of just how
successful we were at making life
redundant, reducing risk and random
occurrence, removing flaws, protecting
nature from its unpredictable chaotic self,
perfecting nature as complement to our
sheer willingness to prevent death and
not realising the irony.

End of the Anthropocene

by Jeremy Cantor

The evolution of our skills outpaced
the evolution of our judgement, so

here we are employing those collective
skills by leaping head-first from the cliff's edge

all together (nearly all together —
some did not come freely to the edge

and needed to be pushed or pulled or shackled
to each other or to us or both),

accelerating toward the rocks below
(at rates we have the skills to calculate),

placing bets (with odds we have the skills
to calculate) on who will live the longest.

Eco Warrior finds the Future as Promised
by Peter Hague

I was green in nineteen-seventy-two.
I'm not green now and know too much.

There was still time then, but none were listening.
Now there's no time and no one is listening.

Experts talk in terms of warnings,
but only from a standpoint of accepted decimation.

There is no measure of attempted avoidance –
humans expand into one, brutal nation.

Animals and landscapes are labelled 'endangered' –
ushered into the memories of a broken planet.

Yet they continue to star in films and photographs –
a foolish compensation for those who care.

A worrying alternative for the predicted extinct,
said by some – and by those visual gamers –

to be available forever
on a hard drive marked: 'nature'.

Waiting for Worms
by Kim M. Russell

After rain, the snow has melted;
in hedges and by the roadside,
beer cans, plastic cups and wrappers explode
like mutated flowers and, in isolated places,
fly-tippers' gifts of mattresses and fridges are exposed.
On the other side of the world,
rare creatures perish, some with pelts,
horns and other parts removed,
waiting for worms to consume
the vestiges of their existence.
Humans' degradation is obscene
while Mother Nature tries to keep the planet clean.

Just Remember

by Jane Dougherty

Arm in arm beneath the trees
we walk into light, wading
through dark leaves
with the music of stones and late roses
singing with the thrush's voice.

Whisper,
don't disturb the quiet
or drive the peace from my head
where lately shadows have crept.

Ask
where it aches, and I will show you
the bruise and the place where the sea
runs away over livid cliffs
in tongues of red water.

Even dreams are full of blood,
this forest floor soaked,
but the rain will come,
wash it clean,

and the sun will soar
when the days lengthen,
and we remember who made us,
and who holds us in the palm of her hand.

Bandage
by Lou Faber

She wants to know if it is even possible
to make a bandage large enough
to bind the wounds we have inflicted
on a planet which we were told
was ours, over which we were
to exercise our wise dominion.

She says it isn't fair that she will be
left to try to clean up the mess
that we have made for it was our
world too, though she adds, we were
not very good at sharing with others.

I want to apologize and tell her
that she is right, that we adults
have failed her generation but
I know she won't believe me, for,
we could have stopped this, but we

always looked out for ourselves
always wanted just a bit more
always were too busy to notice
assumed the others would handle it
said there was nothing we could do.

We hope one day you will
forgive us although we have done
nothing to merit any absolution.

Some Kind of Blue
by Cara Feral

He liked it straight, no chaser please
in '59, shit was bad but not like today
bleached, broken and blanched reefs
Lagan jilted mermaids' love for sale
single use straws stabbed floating
athwart in bleeding nostrils of turtles
like fading trumpet diminuendos
choked by islands of buoyant trash

A bitch's brew of trilling jetsam
strangulated, dappled, and bruised
like the distended neck of Shiva
after drinking our ocean's poison
or the attenuated whispering sustain
of a Miles' trumpet phrased thisness
accompanied to solos of dead species
blown lipped and extinct in a silent way

Bye bye blackbirds' tummies of Coke caps
oil covered pelicans snatch pill bottles
amidst rancid floating piles of garbage
bellies of whales stuffed full of plastic
listen to the trammeled song of crabbers
ladybirds cull through their murky wake
their brass squawks mourn by the fantails
blue in green haze turns sea sickened jade

Electric red tides swell then hip-skit
like the way Bill Evans' fingers moved
six pack wrapped and bound rostrums
parbuckled across green dolphin straits
rotting on lazarets from trawlers' drift nets
the devil may care for sharks caught
tangled up, breathless and sapphirine
split open and bleeding some kind of blue

chapbook menu
by grapeling

the bones of lies stack like paper,
like a chapbook menu

clapped cover to cover
with the ink-blood of failure

etched in slithering rhyme
or discordant reason.

"I am the sea.
Eat me."

I am the soup of your dreams
if your dreams last one-hundred-million years.

perhaps sharks will swim
again in the seventh evolution.

Empty Blue

by Emine Beasley

Into empty blue I stare.
My gaze drowns, bubbles on the surface,
no air.

The last fish was pulled from the ocean today,
a few years before the predicted 2048.
The ecosystem collapsed, our oxygen depleting.
If only we'd known...
But we did know, mistakes repeating.

We had the chance to stop this despair
but instead
into empty blue I stare.

Sweeney The Ghost Shark
by David Cohea

Into my nightly barrow
I harrowed, knelt to pray
my soul to moult
and lay down to sleep

Penzance to dream
the feathered billows of the sea:
Thus engraved the night

took wing and traveled far
beyond all coasts of sight,
that bourne beyond
where starlight rims

a silver door the god
had opened for my dream's
long shark-skeined snout

for reaving noctilucent grail,
diving down with powered tail.
He bid me find the forest
beneath the one I forage

for my spirit's esplumoir,
the chapel down under
my treetop walks inspire.
But the canopy was headless

and burnt in eldritch rows.
The sharks were finless
rounding in ghost spirals.

And the capital of dead coral
was wound by sheeting jellies,
votives of acid nunneries.

Bear this a voice whispered
in my waking ear
I rose an unfinned man
unmoored by deep shark tears
my wings snapping to the
sound of empty seas onshore,
my song their sharkless score.

Tears
by Kim M. Russell

Whale song and tears
trickle through nets otherwise empty.
Over the years,
plastic has filled the space
where sea creatures swam free;
turtles eat mock jellyfish
and drown in melancholy.

Jellyfish Jam
by Ingrid Wilson

Jellyfish jam
sugar-coated with spam,
'But I'm already dead'
the jellyfish said:

'I'm your mushroom cloud
polyurethane shroud
and I'm blooming without
while within there's a drought

and it isn't your fault;
it was never your fault:
you were such a success
populating this mess

but I'm taking my leave
there'll be time yet to grieve
for my kind when we're gone
and the ocean's forlorn.

But your doubts and your fears
can you drown them with tears?
Like you've drowned your own kind
I'd say, time out of mind.

Jellyfish jam
still I am what I am
as I just before said
I am already dead.'

Sea crow
by Kim Whysall-Hammond

Slumping cliffs have thrown down fossiliferous slabs
ancient sea creatures now inhabit the beach

Sea bleached tree trunks lie amongst them
others hang loosely from low crumbly cliffs

Tidal pools sit snug against curving rock ridges
that arc repeatedly across the long beach

A heron fishes from a pool near heavy waves
throws gulls into noisy angry confusion

Along the tide line flies a crow, ragged
with sea wind, damp from spray

A shadow against pale seabirds
she perches on dead white wood

Darkness writ upon the sun bright shore
she flees empty woods, dry fields

Black flag flapping
death's harbinger

The Crow and the Lime Green Plastic Egg
by Jim Feeney

there's a crow
black against the snow
pecking at a lime green plastic egg
down by Jericho Beach Park

the egg will not crack

frustrated,
the crow grabs the egg in its beak
flies to the top of a tree
drops the egg
and flies back down to check its status
the crow repeats this sequence
a number of times

the egg will not crack

the lifetime of a crow
is approximately eight years
the lifetime of a lime green plastic egg
is approximately five hundred years

the egg, therefore, will outlast the crow
the best we can hope for
is that the crow is laying down
some kind of evolutionary marker
one that establishes for future crows
that not all objects
shaped like eggs
are actual eggs

a woman scurries by
wearing a long black hooded coat
the hood obscures her face
she appears to be on an urgent mission

the crow turns from the egg
and cackles:
Where's your scythe, Mrs. Death,
where's your scythe?
You can't do grim, if you don't have a sickle
if you don't have a scythe.
Where's your scythe, Mrs. Death,
where's your scythe?

The magpie sings

by Sarah Connor

One for sorrow. You know me. I'm the bone-
marked, evil bird. You bow to me
if you should see me when I'm all alone,
to turn away misfortune, pay the fee.
Don't forget, though, two for joy –
you never call me lucky. Three
for a girl, four for a boy –
nest-plunderer, fledgling killer – yes, that's me
and five for silver, all those sparkly things,
you say I steal them. Six for gold,
you hoard it up in necklaces and rings.
Seven. The song is done, the secret's told –
Thief. Killer. Evil. That's how you accuse me,
but all these crimes are yours, humanity.

Ancestry
by Kim Whysall-Hammond

Water's polished surface bursts a frog,
bulbous eyes stare boldly into mine
their black depths from an amphibian past
connect to my hind brain, bring silky thoughts,
fluidities and reasons lost to our furry light.

Genome memories from past millennia
the flutter of tadpoles against moist skin
outdistancing sibling predators
the long reach of a tongue curling around dinner
deep time inscribed in neural pathways
while springing between moistures.

Anthropic Demise
by Paul Vincent Cannon

My hand basket caught
fire from fossil fictions as I slid
down the age of denial and
into a carbon copy of the real,
now pale, comparison of
smudged blue planet,
where we swapped diversity
for aesthetics, we trammelled
the soil to pathways of
degradation and choked
every breathing thing to
blackness, now, as I burn,
as earth burns, I know I
shall never again walk
through this rising hell
that we paved with
greedy intentions.

The Fossil Record
by Lou Faber

It should give you pause
to consider that, in the midst
of boundless greed, enmeshed
in the near cult of self, rushing
always to go nowhere quickly,
certain the problems of the world,
can be solved tomorrow, using
resources that may never be
replenished or substituted for,

when we are dead and buried,
we will be the fossil fuels
the future generations
rightfully shun in horror.

PART II

Towards Hope...

A poem for Sherry
by Sarah Connor

hard to think about gifts
and then the starlings come
scattered like letters
on a page, moving like words
forming phrases

the rustle of pages

hard to think about gifts
and then your words
like birds coming
carrying weather
on their wings,
the change of seasons
the slow roll from winter
into spring

the migration of birds
is an act of hope

Heron
by Sherry Marr

The spruce that was your home
got cleared to make way for
a larger heli-pad,
replacing the leafy grove
with a concrete moonscape.
Now I watch you fly over Sobo's,
looking like a skinny matron
with a pocketbook tucked under your wing.

You perch, first here, then there,
trying out new hemlock and cedar spires,
surveying new vistas,
as unsettled as I am,
making yet another move
in my old age.

The trees are coming down
in Clayoquot Sound,
in the UNESCO biosphere reserve
where one would think
they'd be the most protected.

"Progress!" the voices cry.
"Development! You can't stop it."

But we can try.

These tree beings are our lungs,
we plead, we sigh. The planet is
melting; it is burning.
As entangled as you
in the fragility and unraveling
of everything I love
am I.

Invocation of the Trees
by Kerfe Roig

Have mercy on us
we who are poor in spirit
we who are never satisfied
we who strive to possess everything

We who are poor in spirit
bless us and teach us
we who strive to possess everything
fill us as vessels with the breath of stars

Bless us and teach us
cleanse and heal our weary hearts
fill us as vessels with the breath of stars
attach our roots with grace and truth

Cleanse and heal our weary hearts
quench our hunger with light
attach our roots with grace and truth
you who honor both heavens and earth

Quench our hunger with light
we who are never satisfied
you who honor both heavens and earth
have mercy on us

Truth is in
by Jane Dougherty

wrens and robins skirmishing about the house
and honeysuckle in December flower,
sunlight reaching warm fingers across the frost,
tree roots digging deep,
stream-babble.

Listen to the tread of your feet,
stop in the silence,
watch what falls, what rises.

This world washed clean of fear of what is not,
is the world that lives, says the earthworm.

Let the dead hang on their trees,
hide in their seabound caves, tossing fire and plague
or magic words to hold back floods.
Look deep and high,
bird-see,
hare-listen,
sniff the air.

Believe in fingers delved into loose earth
that find the only truths.
Worms are the beginning and the end;
forever bites the tail of never.

Know this,
accept, and live
in bright bird-sweep.

Sweeney's Delight
by David Cohea

Then comes a tree
not for the mad or aggrieved
but strong and spilled from
time's fruitful sleeve;

A sycamore, say, tall
at first light with leaves
big as a girl's head
catching the breeze
in branching sheaves—

scenting first of day
with a most welcome
trace, perfumed by the
god in the tree whose
train is Sweeney's,

exiled from a faith, yes,
but embraced by that green
which wakens the dead
from their drifting dream.

O to hear leaves rattle
for an ecstatic pause—
a shimmering harvest
dancing its applause.

O Niniane enchanted.

A majesty because.

The Sycamores of Sweet Street
by Lisa Fox

Lovingly I see you, sycamores of Sweet Street.
You flow along as kin to build a canopy.
Mottled skin and royal crown, side to side and down,
who could be beneath your boughs and consider
frowns?
Along the blocks we stroll, in perfect shade of thee.

Looking up are jewels of light between your leaves,
sparkling bright with patterns, soft grey skin with
weaves.
Autumn brings your seed pods, dear dangling prickly
rounds,
dear sycamores of Sweet Street.

You trees have been here. So have we. As we shall be,
in peace on Earth. We share our space as we live,
breathe.
Ecosystems network expanding life abounds,
thriving under heaven's grace, sunshine, and the clouds.
Your sacredness gives us blessings; we protect you and
are free,
dear sycamores of Sweet Street.

The Yearning of Blooming Roses
by Linda Lee Lyberg

"A rose in a desert can only survive on its strength, not its beauty."
— Matshona Dhliwayo

A hazy sky yet the sun shines
through filtered gray
as if the earth is weeping
from troubles of this day
the only bells ringing
are tubular chimes singing
tempted and teased
by a lingering western breeze

Their crisp song carries across
a pristine kelly green lawn
to blooming roses yearning
to hear lightness of laughter
in the empty garden–
crystal glasses clinking
and soft murmurs of love
dancing on winter's air
but here only silence reigns

More than yellow blooms on a tree
by Amber Fields

They come to me as ethereal offerings and conviction,
blooms, these blooms
cloaked in understanding,
in dire need of the earth and its beings,
will you commit your name in poetic whispers?
More than yellow blooms on a tree,
I fell asleep unknowingly beneath their shade,
as slowly
the season turns,
you, but closer
those feelings that we are sometimes too afraid to de-
fine;
come, lay your palm upon my chest
and listen,
listen to the thundering of centuries,
can you hear their emerald waters and plea?
Fistful of hair
and silence of night, surrounding—we are moonlight
dressed to approach the earth in pairs,
in pairs
that leave without an explanation,
come, let us bring change,
come let us do things worth our while,
lest we are remembered as ghosts of a dream bygone.

Save our friend Earth

by Benji (Aged 8)

Our earth is very lovely
but oil and smoke
yuck yuck yuck!

We could save our friend Earth
if we use less oil and smoke.
This is no joke.

Oh, great Earth
we will try and save you
because we love you
dear friend Earth
oh yes, we do!

Joy
by Sherry Marr

Joy
comes with the news that Tahlequah,
the mother orca who carried
her dead calf on her nose
for seventeen days, in grief,
two years ago,
has safely delivered her new calf,
who is "healthy and precocious."

Joy is her mother's heart
that, this time, against all odds,
her baby lives.

The Weight of Roses After Rain
by Linda Lee Lyberg

When winter rains dampen terra firma
earthy petrichor perfume fills sultry air
I wander out to my untamed garden
to see what surprises await there

Wildflower seeds have sprouted up
breaking through rich sandy loam
lavender spikes burgeoning forth
reaching for now absent sun

But for me there is nothing much sweeter
than the heavy scent of roses after rain
with fragrant petals tenderly weeping
from feeling all humanity's pain

The Last Mohican and the Last Tree
by Ivor Steven

Where is that green mythical memory lane
our planet's last vestige of living wood grain
I see an earthy trail between golden fern rails
overshadowed by ancient black forest sails

where a preserving fog shrouds the secret entrance
sheltering nature's life-giving trees from human ascen-
dance
a sanctuary, safe from finality, unlike the last *Mohican*
a surviving jungle canopy, like a *Lost World's* beacon

Leaves Fall to Moulder
by RedCat

Leaves fall to moulder, the veils thin
spirits approaching, the haunting fog flows in
time to remember, where we begin
where we want to, and where we have been

Spirits approaching, the haunting fog flows in
full of visions, every dream and sin
where we want to, and where we have been
who has hurt you, who's a spiritual twin

Full of visions, every dream and sin
to grow and evolve, that's the goal, not to win
who has hurt you, who's a spiritual twin
find those who nurture the passion within

To grow and evolve, that's the goal, not to win
leaves fall to moulder, the veils thin
find those who nurture the passion within
time to remember, where we begin

Between
by Kerfe Roig

The path connects the path divides,
the sky is rising like a tree—
the ending moves, retreats, and hides
what is, is not, has yet to be.

The sky is rising like a tree,
the land grows, following behind
what is, is not, has yet to be—
an offering returned in kind.

The land grows, following behind
the dance of water, spirits, earth—
an offering returned in kind—
a trance, a dream, remembered birth.

A dance of water, spirits, earth—
the ending moves, retreats and hides
a trance, a dream, remembered birth—
the path connects the path divides.

In reply to 'Between' by Kerfe Roig
by Amber Fields

I see you across the dunes, across the land that grows,
like violet rain that pours
my hands are drawn to you without trace of qualm, of
doubt.
The sky is, the sky was,
the sky has always been known to keep its promises,
rosier than rose
these feelings swapping between sugar and sorrow,
the spaces between our fingers where hope flows—can
you
honestly say that you have never felt this way before?
Pull me down to your depths, earth
and teach me the art of bleeding light into the cracks at
dawn,
today,
the beating of my lover's heart beckons to me, come
vacancies of rain
yielding to tender ground, even in fragments
let us choose to understand, let us choose to understand;
your bosom, earth, no longer parched with waiting.

This Place
by Lisa Fox

At the earth's edge there is water,
and from water we see the earth.
Two elements, united by the wind.
Congregated by amorphous clouds
is the infinite blueness of the sky.
The majesty sets our minds on fire.

At sunset is the gleaming brilliance of fire.
Red lights the ripples of dark water,
saturates every bit of the sky,
and paints wet objects on the earth;
it tinges even the clouds,
whose sheen shifts with the wind.

On quiet mornings there is no wind.
We see a hemisphere of fire
with no hint in the air of clouds,
rising, silently, over the water,
above the blackness of the earth.
A new dawn is beginning in the sky.

On the mountain top, all is sky.
We are close companions of the wind.
Far below us we see glimpses of earth;
here and there, below, lights as fires.
The lakes look like tiny puddles of water.
We see eye to eye with the clouds.

Birds roll and tumble in the clouds.
As lakes for us, they swim in the sky.
Their somersaults and dives, reflected in the water,
maneuvering with swells of the wind,
red feathers in the sun, fire on fire;
nature's magnificent show above the earth.

Above the core and the rocks is the earth,
which is an orienting presence for the clouds,
which is alive with life, and sustains beyond fire.
It shares Gaia with the sky,
is shifted by the wind,
and is carried down mountains with water.

Water is Father, Mother is Earth
Wind is Sister, Brothers are Clouds
Sky is Wise, Great Illuminator is Fire.

Like Breathing
by Kerfe Roig

Black is the color of creation.
The void is beginning.
Emptiness must be filled.
You can't have something without nothing.

And how does that apply to imaginary beings?
Must there also be a counterpart that's real?

Must every question have an answer and every answer a
question?

Catch the words—
in context they become magic.
Recreate the patterns that create potential,
the map to being born.

A cloud is like breathing.
Breathing is like catching.
Catching is like stopping time.
Stopping time is like an earthquake.
An earthquake is like a heart beating fast.
A heart beating fast is like drumming.
Drumming is like dancing.
Dancing is like a bird.
A bird is like flowers.
Flowers are like a rainbow.
A rainbow is like a song.
A song is like the universe.
The universe is like a wheel.

The void is pregnant.

The journey is alive.

Do we get broken so we can be fixed?

Buried reality
by Rishika Jain (Aged 13)

We're all humans, aren't we?
We feel and think and have hearts as pure as nature's
beauty.
Then why is it that everywhere I turn, I find my heart
trapped with thoughts that I dread?
Why do I find myself caged with emotions of words
unsaid?

Look back. Could you have been kinder to that old lady
asking for directions?
More considerate while throwing trash in the middle
of the road, leaving it to drivers' inconvenience and the
workman's misery?
More thoughtful while dirtying the world, regardless of
the repercussions and domino effect caused by a simple
act of idiocy?

In the end, can it hurt to be a little kinder?
You might help someone, keep them from falling apart
so why would you sit back
while you can mend a broken heart?

Just a tiny act of goodness
for the greater good
leads to a change
that I hope you've understood.

Mother of Creation
by RedCat

Ruler of life's seasons
Keeper of moon tides
Guardian of love's reasons
Champion of hidden pride

Teacher of passion
Wellspring of lust
Star of heaven
Lodestone of trust

Spinner of transformation
Pollinator of hope
Mother of creation
Thy wisdom we invoke

Mercy 1 and 2 (after M L Smoker)
by Kerfe Roig

An answer arrives,
but it's not words,
not even something
that you can hear.

—not that you
ever listen to anything
anyway—
How do you
recognize it?—
but you know
that your inside has shifted
into what it wasn't—

At the same time
you are still where you were—
you still face towards impossibility
in every direction—

And yet your mind is not the same—
a strange memory you cannot name
has cleared a path between
the synapses of despair
and you can breathe again.

Is the light lost?
You leave a candle burning,
place it in the window–
come home

Leave a light footprint
by Ingrid Wilson

Leave a light footprint:
tread softly on your way
go with grace and dignity and always
with a light step
with a light heart
without a thought
of waste
or want
or wishing more than plenty;
seeking only
harmony
take nothing more than what you give.

Leave a light footprint:
one day
your children
will follow in the steps you leave behind
leave them a clear path
and a safe route
to a bright future;
turn off the light on your way out
that they may shine the brighter.

Leave a light footprint,
even as you take your
leave
a deep impression on the hearts
of those you love.

Printed in Great Britain
by Amazon